Echoes

A Collection of Linked-Verse Poetry

Michelle Hyatt & Jacob Salzer

2020

This book is dedicated to:

Mother Earth

To all kind people

To *you*

Echoes

ISBN: 978-1-716-41079-6

Echoes: A Collection of Linked-Verse Poetry

A Lulu Publication | www.lulu.com

Acknowledgments

I would like to acknowledge the poets from Haiku Nook G+, who inspired me to stretch my edges and explore the endless possibilities in creating tiny poems. I am forever grateful for their kindness and friendship.

I would also like to give many thanks to Jacob, who not only continues to be a wonderful teacher, but a trusted and treasured friend.

And last but never least, I give deepest honour to my dad, who showed me from my earliest beginnings the sacredness of the Wild World. Papa, I feel you everywhere.

Michelle Hyatt

I would like to thank all the great poets who have gone before us, who have left behind linked-verse poetry that continues to inspire us to write and collaborate.

I would also like to thank Willie R. Bongcaron for creating Haiku Nook G+. Thanks to Haiku Nook G+, I had the chance to meet poets around the world and edit our Haiku Nook anthologies, *Yanty's Butterfly* and *Half A Rainbow*. Through international correspondence and sharing haiku, I became a much better writer and editor.

I would like to thank Shelley Baker-Gard and Carolyn Winkler for founding the Portland Haiku Group.

I would like to thank Clayton Beach, the linked-verse editor at *Under the Basho*, for publishing linked-verse poetry.

I also would like to thank Garry Gay for inventing rengay and Michael Dylan Welch for writing the first rengay with Garry in 1992 that led to many other collaborations.

I would like to give a special thanks to Michelle Hyatt for her friendship, her kindness, and her deep connections to the Earth.

Lastly, I would like to thank my family for everything they have done and continue to bring to life.

Jacob Salzer

Contents

Introduction

Echoes is a collection of linked-verse poetry by Michelle Hyatt and Jacob Salzer created over the course of a year through email correspondence.

We honor the traditional forms of linked-verse poetry and those who have gone before us. As such, we have done our very best to stay true to the traditional forms while allowing some room for experimentation. As an example, in our two-line verses, sometimes there is an ellipsis within one line. We also wrote experimental six-link rengay, where our verses link-and-shift within broader, abstract themes. We've also included tan renga sequences. As a reference, we primarily used John Carley's book, *Renku Reckoner*.

In terms of linked-verse forms, our book consists of tan renga sequences, yotsumono, rengay, experimental six-link rengay, junicho, a kasen, and solo linked-verse.

Our names, themes, and publication credits are located in the back of the book. This allows each piece to be read without distraction or additional text.

Ultimately, *Echoes* is a book of friendship. In the spirit of friendship, Michelle and I encourage you to write collaboratively to break down the walls of solitary writing and make new friends and connections.

We've also provided linked-verse journals and resources at the back of our book to read more about rengay and the many different forms of renku.

Safe travels. We hope you enjoy the journey!

Michelle Hyatt & Jacob Salzer

Echoes

Tan Renga Sequences

Past Lives

past lives
the ancestors smile
in my grandma's face

dry river bed
the thirst for knowledge

***

smile lines
at the labyrinth...
a soft breeze

in the maze... the end
is the beginning

***

buried treasure
the untold stories
of our elders

shipwreck...
shadows in the wind

Unspoken Stories

all that's left
of my dream journal
morning rain

pushing through the mud
a single lotus

***

gaps in the conversation
the homeless man's
missing teeth

unspoken stories...
hiding behind a forced smile

***

teaching me
to be still...
deep forest

my chanting becomes
evening birdsong

Yotsumono

Early Spring

all that's left
of the outdoor concert
crickets

fading spiral…
a veery sings at twilight

reincarnation
empty snail shells
in father's garden

steady breath - from Gaia's belly
a white lily

An Old Village

pausing
on the garden path
blue hydrangeas

liminal space...the brush between
an artist and his canvas

an old village
in the silence of a deep valley
trees in moonlight

a shadow dips in the rain barrel
Po Po's bamboo cup

Shadow

hunter's moon
the deer walks
into a shadow

grandpa's forest path
buried under leaves

hidden eyes—
tunnelling vibrations
of a black mole

evening tide in C minor
the dissonance of stars

North Wind

old sheepskin mukluks
dreams of snowshoeing
covered in dust

grandma's ashes merge
into the river, into the sea

crystalline silence
in a midwinter's forest
your warm embrace

moonlight on broken ice
the buds of yellow roses

Rengay

Perseverance

running uphill
the final stretch
of a marathon

temple steps...the beads of sweat
to purification

upstream
rainbow trout jump
into pools of light

roots and shoots...
push-pull energy
in a garden

cracks in the sidewalk—
trees rise above hospital windows

axial extension
making room to breathe
from tailbone to crown

Crescendo

sound check
at an outdoor concert
the buzz of energy

tuning the electric guitar...
a stream of sunlight

mood adjustment
a slow crescendo
practicing scales

silhouettes ascending
the subway stairs...
trumpet solo

on Broadway - walking past
dreams of every busker

closed record shop
The Dark Side of the Moon
still spinning

A Single Match

a single match
newspaper articles bend
into flames

turning up the heat
sizzle sounds in a frying pan

grandpa's wood stove
smoke evaporates
into the Milky Way

fireworks show
I lean my head further back
in the oak chair

coal mine explosion—
the buried hum of electricity

faulty wire
replacing a table lamp
with candles

The Machine

the rise and fall
of my checking account
evening tide

another recession- making ends meet
moonlighting

rugged mountain trail
the steady climb
to retirement

nest egg
finding the balance
of work and pleasure

capitalism—
a weathered fence covered in snow

white concrete
beside a squatter village
mansions

A Steady Pulse

hill running
the challenge of ascending
a resistant mind

slowly hiking a forest trail
the distant rapids

single kayak
each stroke sinking deeper
in her core

mountain wind...
everyone in the yoga class
stands still

deep breath
the blissful silence of ecstatic dance

tai chi...
the steady pulse
of the sea

Gravity

one apple
setting the world in motion
a sudden wind

the cosmic bowling ball
spins into darkness

heavy silence
beneath a new moon
high tide

tossing a coin
into the empty well...
his wish

dreams descending into echoes...
my father's voice

an icicle
in the deep cave
her promise

A Drop of Water

drum circle
the reverberation
of thunder

flash flood
gathering yesterday's plastic

moonlit river
the flow of a conversation
between strangers

summer kiss
the waterfall's mist suspended
in a breeze

echoing in a tunnel
a drop of water

dark rain
never forgotten
Hiroshima...

First Flight

growing season
a robin feeds her fledglings
in the garden

mowing father's lawn...
the blue heron's shadow

zentangle sky
a murmuration
of starlings

seeking refuge
the crow disappears
into a maple tree

vision quest
an eagle takes flight

a silence
between strangers... the blur
of a hummingbird

Kaleidoscope

closed umbrella...
a ladybug rests
on a milkweed leaf

peering into a kaleidoscope
the butterfly's eyes

forest run
matching the cadence
of katydids

darkness...
a withered field swarms
with fireflies

campfire stories
the distant sound of crickets

her transparency...
sunlight filters through
the dragonfly's wings

Experimental Rengay

Inheritance

whispers
through the branches...
my mother's voice

catkins blowing in the breeze
an orb spider weaves her web

grandma's blanket...
I wrap myself
in silence

in the ancient ways
you teach me to walk
lightly...

stairs spiraling into darkness...
the roots of my family tree

buried bones
deep inside the earth
a faint vibration

Life Cycles

evening tide
a new song recedes
into the past

temple bell
a monk checks his phone

grandma peers
into her grandchild's eyes
crescent moon

unwritten stories...
a pubescent girl packs away
her fairy tales

first day of history class
the weight of his textbook

she laughs through tears
blowing and catching
yesterday's kisses

Unbeaten Path

unbeaten path...
helping my mother settle in
a nursing home

beneath the giant oak tree
a leaf falls without a sound

leaving behind
memories of yesterday
rock collection

roaring waterfall
we hike past
muffled voices

rustling in the night
a deer beds down alone

rays of moonlight
in a deepening silence...
our footsteps

The Labyrinth

steep forest trail
father and I slowly climb
into morning mist

a cloud of stillness falls
on the summit of Haleakala

quiet after rain...
a deep lake fills
with stars

night air
tingling against my skin
the warmth of your hands

campfire stories...
headlines rise into moonlight

crickets
our thoughts become
one vibration

Remnants of a Dream

in the gap
between waking and sleeping
morning rain

an ethereal voice whispers...
dreams of flying

geese migration
I readjust the feathers
in my pillow

a soft breeze...
the quiet fluttering
of rapid eye movement

tratak meditation—
the flame burns into darkness

twilight's last shadow
surrendering attachment
to the light

Final Frontier

static sound...
my radio becomes
a tricorder

compounding data
the memory of a star

a black cloak
hovering in space
the bird of prey

digital eyes
orbiting the earth...
Google satellites

a probe calls to whales
on the brink of extinction

Spock raises an eyebrow
the sound of water
on Andoria

Summer's Passage

afternoon picnic
drinking wine on a blanket
bees in red clover

between threads of conversation
the taste of honey

a warm kiss
spreading bare toes deeper
in the sand

sunset...
the ocean leaves behind
polished stones

childhood memories...the fireflies
play hide and seek

the summer moon
glimpsed behind drifting clouds
her secrets

Autumn Harvest

all that's left
of the family potluck
a trail of ants

suffonsified smiles at the table…
a collective burp

a small earthquake…
with a potato in her hand
the farmer listens

churning soil
the worms burrow deeper…
autumn harvest

still shadows… a graveyard
covered in leaves

slow burning candles
savouring the silence
while our tea steeps

Genesis

in the beginning
creation sparkles
on blades of grass

photosynthesis... the first bacteria
swimming in the sea

light energy
igniting the breath...
sun salutations

power outage—
the silence fills
with birdsong

tinging cutlery...
laughter at a family breakfast

garden bed
she buries the seed
of a dream

Wandering

on the Rhine River
ruins of a castle
soaked in sunlight

kings and queens in the Great Pyramid
red hieroglyphs

drenched stop sign
after the Alabama storm
waves of humidity

sea smells
under Galata Bridge
eating balik ekmek

moonlight on Takhlakh Lake
my friend's shadow

paper lanterns
in Peace Park...we remember
Hiroshima

Ripple Effect

epiphany—
a cloud turns
into an afro

dreadlocks in an ocean breeze...
the sailor's knot

bean curry...
a fart ripples across
the meditation room

asana practice
in low-rise yoga pants
half moon

twilight zone at the store...
where is the toilet paper?

public announcement
in every aisle
my squeaky shoes

Road Trip

smooth highway
the satellite radio
preset for jazz

bumps on the gravel road
grandpa's stories

travelling back
to an old country town
lost in time

rusted yellow paint
on a crowded school bus
children chatting

joyful smiles
in a field of sunflowers

dusk
between garden stone walls
their first kiss

Resurrection

sacred drum
following the rhythm
of Grandmother Moon

monks chant in a circle
om mane padme hum

minaret
the oak trees rustle
a call to prayer

Zen garden...
by the Buddha statue
a deeper silence

Heel Stone shadows lengthen
summer solstice

resurrection
sea fog slowly rising
into stars

Junicho

Southern Migration

scent of Jasmine
in the garden...two shadows
become still

rain clouds hover above
the Laughing Buddha

hidden faces
in the roaring river...
our ancestors

heavy snow boots - with each step
I see my breath

a long forest trail
breaking the silence between us
my mother's voice

soft candle glow...
a quiet meal we share together

homeless gather
beneath the bridge
sunset

orange hues - the southern migration
of monarch butterflies

a red-tailed hawk
settles on the power line
Autumn moon

aqua yoga
the weight I leave behind

end of summer—
driftwood and stones
buried in sand

life cycles -
directions on the Medicine Wheel

Grandma's Stories

white lilacs
the soft lilt
of a robin's song

spring rain on a tin roof...
doyra drumming

circle dance
from her regalia
the grass speaks

wildflower meadow...
a samurai sword buried in snow

mother's quilt
the lines of her hands
in every star

slowly weaving a basket...
grandma's stories

rattan chair
the art of zazen
in a bamboo forest

old graveyard... a red leaf falls
without a sound

harvest moon
in her womb shadows
a memory ghost

the raspy voice of a farmer
disappearing in the corn field

golden sunset
across the lake - a creaking door
slowly closes

the end of another movie
running in a dream

42

Kasen

First Light

first light
the silent Om
of a white crocus

out of a cracked egg
the blue heron's cry

reunion
an icicle melting
into the soil

the veins of a cedar tree
anchored in darkness

midnight wind chill
a loneliness stalks
the Wolf Moon

drifting snow . . .
the words she left behind

the smell of pencil
on grid-paper blueprints
grandpa's voice

sage smoke rises
remembering the old prayers

campfire embers
she weaves dry grass
into a basket

thread count
flickers in Corona Borealis

thoughts fading . . .
grandma slowly sips
a cup of coffee

hibernal cave
the long pause of a bear's breath

winter evening
drops of moonlight slide down
the cabin window

blank canvas
a young bride adjusts her veil

between movies
on the empty theater screen
my shadow

new release
Mother Earth tilts closer to the sun

baby shower . . .
innumerable plum blossoms
drenched in rain

soft purple ribbons
swirling around the maypole

rainbow flag
letting my hair down
in the wind

outdoor flute concert
two strangers whispering

gentle flutter...
quietly she dreams
of her first love

a wilted rose on the bed
their last kiss

al fresco dining
the intimacy we share
with stillness

the long arc of an arrow
summer sunset

warrior pose
a golden eagle watches
from the mountaintop

white water rapids
the turns in her story

old waltz
graceful breezes arouse
a taiga forest

a trail of dead leaves
my footsteps

a rebirth journey
in every seed
harvest moon

pumpkin candles
I carve into the night

all that's left
of the birthday party . . .
his wish

crystal vibrations...
the steady ticking of time

evening tide . . .
the weathered paint of a ship
buried in sand

Laughing Buddha
robin song in a Zen garden

monastery pond –
the lingering scent
of cherry blossoms

small ripple...
greening worlds begin to stir

Solo Linked-Verse

Great Grandma

in silence
the old woman's head
sinks to her chest

vacant eyes
words escape
great grandma

whispering: be careful
sound of a door closing

telling stories
she stops
mid-sentence

theater of the absurd
she never liked politics

cracking jokes
great grandma laughs
one last time

lights out
the ceiling fan
keeps spinning

Wedding Story

walking briskly down the aisle
a girl fiercely tosses
flower petals

just married
she can't pronounce her last name

trying to speak
another language
the Russian girls giggle

worlds within words
attempting to translate my haiku

tired of the English language
I sit in the shade
with a cranefly

silent flight
the transparent wings of a butterfly

her smile
hidden behind
her wedding dress

a young girl taps the bride's knee
and gives her a dollar

Bottom of the 9th

bottom of the 9th
drops of moonlight
on the pitcher's face

strangers huddled together
without names

fly-out
a baseball player
waves at the moon

under bright lights
the constant hum of conversation

a hushed silence
after the pitcher throws
another strike

SMACK! the baseball disappears
into the crowd

sudden downpour
a thousand pairs of hands
clapping

Black Ice

black ice
I drive over
the moon

vape smoke escapes
her pale white face

early morning
the prisoner's breath lingers
above barbed-wire

tire chains left behind
on the narrow highway

Christmas shopping
she tries on
another necklace

gold light shimmers
across the water

breaking news
in the old t.v.
drifting clouds

trying to sleep
in the hospital lobby

smell of coffee
I take another bite
of a salad

strangers walking briskly
through the garden

receding
deep into the night
sound of sirens

seagulls calling
above dim streetlamps

dementia...
waves washing away
footprints in the sand

migratory patterns
in the wings of a butterfly

check-mate
my neighbor gives me
another cookie

new cracks form
in the marble steps

heavy rain
sunlight pierces through
broken thoughts

solving the last word
of a crossword puzzle

early morning...
I light another journal
on fire

headlines trickle down
a vacant driveway

A Quiet Stream

morning meditation
I breathe
the trees

spring robin
the sun awakens new beginnings

waxing moon
feeling the first flutter
in her belly

a quiet stream…in bubbles
thoughts drift away

river rocks
all my rough edges
smoothed over with time

smile lines
looking through old photo albums

mature forest
the wisdom
of oak trees

Opa's stories…we listen
to the ancestors

cottage memories
laughter of children
chasing fireflies

late night kiss
twinkling stars in our eyes

She

ancient rhythms
dancing around the flame
barefoot women

blood mysteries - glowing from the maiden
a spring moon

sacred circle
our Great Mother
turns the Wheel

driving passion
the haunting howl of a She-wolf

unleashed spirit
a volcano
speaks her truth

wild freedom
True North guiding me home

winter's rest
the quiet abode
of the Crone

grey hair
getting settled with stillness

no resistance
an old stream flows
slow and steady

evening walk along the beach
each step sinking deeper

A Sign of Spring

candlelight dinner
the soft flicker
in your eyes

slow dancing
two shadows become one

Moonlight Sonata
the first time
I notice your hands

andante…our vibration
reaching across the miles

telephone lines
still buzzing
after midnight

time change - the adjustments
after an October wedding

hard climb
enduring ups and downs
rocky terrain

diamond mine - the earth shifts
in another direction

crescent moon
an indent
on my ring finger

cosmic silence
the dark galaxy between us

bridge repair
learning to build
with new tools

friendship
roots that remain in our garden

a green bud
on the apple tree
once thought dead

first robin - hearing my dad's voice
a sign of spring

guardian angels
in the clouds
a dragon and horse

quiet echo
a promise still remembered

A New Day

hidden words
finishing his sentence
with silence

fiction novel - stories of myself
I used to believe

magick show
pole beans sprouting
in the garden

stone pagoda...breaking apart
pictures of kintsugi

imperfection
beautiful colours
outside the lines

inner journey
a map with no destination

a higher love
reflected in a calm lake
trees

holy ground
walking lightly with Gaia

Handel's Messiah
the hallelujah chorus
in birdsong

the Phoenix rising from ashes
a new day

Authors & Publication Credits

Tan Renga Sequences

Page 3, *Past Lives*

Michelle Hyatt – odd verses
Jacob Salzer – even verses

Page 4, *Unspoken Stories*

Jacob Salzer – odd verses
Michelle Hyatt – even verses

Publication credit: *Under the Basho, 2020 – Linked Forms*

Yotsumono (4-link)

Page 7, *Early Spring*

Season: spring

Jacob Salzer – odd verses
Michelle Hyatt – even verses

Page 8, *An Old Village*

Season: summer

Jacob Salzer – odd verses
Michelle Hyatt – even verses

Yotsumono (4-link) (continued)

Page 9, *Shadow*

Season: autumn

Michelle Hyatt – odd verses
Jacob Salzer – even verses

Page 10, *North Wind*

Season: winter

Michelle Hyatt – odd verses
Jacob Salzer – even verses

Rengay (6-link)

Page 13, *Perseverance*

Theme: things rising; elevation; new heights; hiking; climbing; growth

Jacob Salzer – odd verses
Michelle Hyatt – even verses

Page 14, *Crescendo*

Theme: music; concerts/festivals; musicians; instruments; singing; records; radio

Michelle Hyatt – odd verses
Jacob Salzer – even verses

Rengay (6-link) (continued)

Page 15, *A Single Match*

Theme: fire; warmth; heat; cooking; electricity; sun; light; explosions; batteries; powered appliances

Jacob Salzer – odd verses
Michelle Hyatt – even verses

Page 16, *The Machine*

Theme: money; economy; finances; retirement; accounting; jobs; careers

Jacob Salzer – odd verses
Michelle Hyatt – even verses

Page 17, *A Steady Pulse*

Theme: physical fitness; gyms; weight-lifting; cardio health/running; body movement; strength and flexibility; health/healthy living

Michelle Hyatt – odd verses
Jacob Salzer – even verses

Page 18, *Gravity*

Theme: gravity; energy; weight/weightlessness; earth; tide; force - push/pull

Michelle Hyatt – odd verses
Jacob Salzer – even verses

Rengay (6-link) (continued)

Page 19, *A Drop of Water*

Theme: water

Jacob Salzer – odd verses
Michelle Hyatt – even verses

Page 20, *First Flight*

Theme: birds

Michelle Hyatt – odd verses
Jacob Salzer – even verses

Page 21, *Kaleidoscope*

Theme: insects

Michelle Hyatt – odd verses
Jacob Salzer – even verses

Experimental Rengay (6-link)

Page 25, *Inheritance*

Theme: Mother Earth; Trees; the Divine Feminine

Jacob Salzer – odd verses
Michelle Hyatt – even verses

Publication credit: *Under the Basho, 2020 – Linked Forms*

Experimental Rengay (6-link) (continued)

Page 26, *Life Cycles*

Theme: time travel, past & future; imagination & memories; old/ancient & new/modern

Jacob Salzer – odd verses
Michelle Hyatt – even verses

Page 27, *Unbeaten Path*

Theme: hiking/trails/trail blazing/wilderness

Michelle Hyatt – odd verses
Jacob Salzer – even verses

Page 28, *The Labyrinth*

Theme: rising & falling; climbing & descending;
new heights & deeper depths; waves; frequency; voice;
music; vibration

Jacob Salzer – odd verses
Michelle Hyatt – even verses

Page 29, *Remnants of a Dream*

Theme: dreams, sleep, insomnia, meditation, the
subconscious mind

Jacob Salzer – odd verses
Michelle Hyatt – even verses

Experimental Rengay (6-link) (continued)

Page 30, *Final Frontier*

Theme: Star Trek; aliens; spaceships; space travel; planets, galaxies, stars

Michelle Hyatt – odd verses
Jacob Salzer – even verses

Page 31, *Summer's Passage*

Theme: summer; outdoor activities; sunsets; beaches; heat & humidity

Michelle Hyatt – odd verses
Jacob Salzer – even verses

Page 32, *Autumn Harvest*

Theme: food; tea; cooking; gardening; farms; grocery stores; restaurants; potlucks

Jacob Salzer – odd verses
Michelle Hyatt – even verses

Page 33, *Genesis*

Theme: morning; dawn; sunrise; silent space; birdsong; awakening; genesis

Michelle Hyatt – odd verses
Jacob Salzer – even verses

Experimental Rengay (6-link) (continued)

Page 34, *Wandering*

Theme: travel; vacations; foreign languages & places

Jacob Salzer – odd verses
Michelle Hyatt – even verses

Page 35, *Ripple Effect*

Theme: funny moments; respectful humor; unusual moments; light-heartedness; laughter

Jacob Salzer – odd verses
Michelle Hyatt – even verses

Page 36, *Road Trip*

Theme: road trips; day tripping; car travel; small towns; detours; scenic views

Michelle Hyatt – odd verses
Jacob Salzer – even verses

Page 37, *Resurrection*

Theme: prayer; worship; churches, temples, sacred places; spirit; religion; dogma; Divine Form

Michelle Hyatt – odd verses
Jacob Salzer – even verses

Junicho (12-link)

Page 41, *Southern Migration*

Jacob Salzer – odd verses
Michelle Hyatt – even verses

Page 42, *Grandma's Stories*

Michelle Hyatt – odd verses
Jacob Salzer – even verses

Kasen (36-link)

Pages 45-48, *First Light*

First sheet, front (Preface/Jo) (first 6 verses)

Michelle Hyatt – odd verses
Jacob Salzer – even verses

First sheet, back (Development/Ha) (Part 1) (12 verses)

Jacob Salzer – odd verses
Michelle Hyatt – even verses

Second sheet, front (Intensification/Ha) (Part 2) (12 verses)

Michelle Hyatt – odd verses
Jacob Salzer – even verses

Second sheet, back (Finale) (Kyu) (last 6 verses)

Jacob Salzer – odd verses
Michelle Hyatt – even verses

Solo Linked-Verse

Page 51, *Great Grandma* (solo 7-link)

Jacob Salzer – all verses

Publication credit: *Under the Basho, 2019 – Linked Forms*

Page 52, *Wedding Story* (solo 8-link)

Jacob Salzer – all verses

Page 53, *Bottom of the 9th* (solo 7-link)

Jacob Salzer – all verses

Publication credit: *Under the Basho, 2019 – Linked Forms*

Pages 54-55, *Black Ice* (solo 20-link)

Jacob Salzer – all verses

Publication credit: *Under the Basho, 2018 – Linked Forms*

Page 56, *A Quiet Stream* (solo 10-link)

Michelle Hyatt – all verses

Publication credit: *Under the Basho, 2020 – Linked Forms*

Page 57, *She* (solo 10-link)

Michelle Hyatt – all verses

Publication credit: *Under the Basho, 2020 – Linked Forms*

Pages 58-59, *A Sign of Spring* (solo 16-link)

Michelle Hyatt – all verses

Page 60, *A New Day* (solo 10-link)

Michelle Hyatt – all verses

Bios

Michelle Hyatt has been spending time with haiku since 2014. She appreciates the depth and mystery haiku carry, and how they create a space for her to tune into the senses; to feel, and feel, and then feel some more.

Michelle writes haiku for the simple, sheer, creative pleasure. It is truly one of her greatest joys, having also brought healing, growth and friendship. Her haibun, haiku and renku have appeared in *the International Women's Haiku Festival, Contemporary Haibun Online, Modern Haiku, Frogpond* and *Under the Basho*, and the international publications *Yanty's Butterfly: Haiku Nook: An Anthology* and *Half a Rainbow: Haiku Nook: An Anthology*.

Soulcraft is expressed in many of Michelle's passions, some of which include reading, painting and drawing, creating Nature arts and crafts, gardening, running, archery, paddleboarding and kayaking, cross-country skiing and snowshoeing, playing guitar and the frame drum, singing and dancing, yoga and other forms of meditation, and spending time with family and friends.

Michelle is a certified health and wellness coach, yoga and meditation teacher. She lives in breath-taking Northern Ontario, Canada with her devoted husband, brilliant children, and gorgeous dog.

"This is how you change the world, the smallest circles first… That humble energy, the kind that says, 'I will do what I can do right now in my own small way,' creates a ripple effect on the world."

~ Richard Wagamese, *One Drum: Stories and Ceremonies for a Planet*

Jacob Salzer has been writing haiku and related forms since 2006, when he took a haiku class at The Evergreen State College: *The Way of Haiku and Haibun* taught by Kate Crow. Since that time, Jacob has published his haiku, tanka, and haibun in numerous journals, and has published 4 collections of haiku, 1 collection of tanka, 1 collection of haibun, and 1 collection of longer poems, *The Last Days of Winter*.

Jacob served as the managing editor of two Haiku Nook anthologies: *Yanty's Butterfly* (dedicated to haiku poet Yanty Tjiam) and *Half A Rainbow* (dedicated to haiku poet Rachel Sutcliffe). Jacob is also an active member of the Portland Haiku Group, where he served as the managing editor of the Portland Haiku Group anthology, *New Bridges*, dedicated to haiku poet Johnny Baranski. He is currently editing another Haiku Nook international haiku anthology, *Desert Rain*.

Jacob enjoys spending time with his friends and family and has several interests, including: painting, drawing, photography, music, poetry, meditation, exercise, nutrition, neurobiology, medical coding, reading, editing, professional networking, and social activism. As a musician, he enjoys playing piano, guitar and tabla drums from India. He frequently utilizes the *Americans of Conscience checklist* (https://americansofconscience.com/) to advocate for a better U.S. and world. Inspired by the Great Seal of the United States, *E Pluribus Unum*, a latin phrase that translates to: Out of Many, One, Jacob values respect and diversity, and is dedicated to creating new bridges and community in a world that far too often appears violent and fragmented.

Jacob frequently writes about water and his favorite color is blue. His newest collection, *Mare Liberum* is a cumulation of his haiku and tanka inspired by water and the sea.

Resources

Journals that publish linked-verse

Under the Basho

https://www.underthebasho.com/submission/linked-form-submissions.html

Ephemerae

https://ephemeraejournal.blogspot.com/2018/03/ephemerae-print-journal-for-haikai.html

Failed Haiku

https://failedhaiku.com/submissions-guidelines/

Frogpond

http://www.hsa-haiku.org/frogpond/submissions.html

Haiku Canada Review

https://haikucanada.org/home/publications.php?page=1003

Hedgerow

https://hedgerowhaiku.com/submissions/

Journals that publish linked-verse (continued)

Mariposa

https://www.hpnc.org/mariposa

Presence

https://haikupresence.org/contribute

Prune Juice

https://prunejuice.wordpress.com/submissions/

Wales

https://www.waleshaikujournal.com/submit

Chrysanthemum

http://chrysanthemum-haiku.net/en/submission-
guidelines.html

Education

GraceGuts by Michael Dylan Welch

http://www.graceguts.com/rengay

http://www.graceguts.com/rengay-essays

http://www.graceguts.com/collaborations

Book Recommendations

Renku Reckoner, John Carley (Darlington Richards Press, 2015)

Japanese Linked Poetry, Earl Miner (Princeton University Press, 1979)